THE ABORIGINAL TRIBES OF THE NILGIRI HILLS

THE ABORIGINAL TRIBES OF THE NILGIRI HILLS

W. ROSS KING

GYAN

Published by

GYAN

Gyan Publishing House
5, Ansari Road
Daryaganj, New Delhi-110002
Phone: 011-47034999, 9811692060
E-mail: books@gyanbooks.com

Distribution Network
gyanbooks.com
India, USA, Canada, UK, Australia

ISBN: 978-93-7225-664-2 (HB)

First Published, 1870

2nd Impression 2025

Printed at: Gyan Press, Delhi.

THE ABORIGINAL TRIBES OF THE NILGIRI HILLS
Author: W. ROSS KING

TODA WOMAN.

TODA MAN

THE

ABORIGINAL TRIBES

OF

THE NILGIRI HILLS.

BY

LIEUT.-COLONEL W. ROSS KING, F.R.G.S., F.S.A.S.,
ETC.

A Paper read before the Anthropological Society of London, May 3, 1870, *and published by the Society in the Journal of Anthropology.*

LONDON:
LONGMANS, GREEN, AND Co.
1870.

THE

ABORIGINAL TRIBES OF THE NILGIRI HILLS.

BY

LIEUT.-COLONEL W. ROSS KING, F.R.G.S., F.S.A.S., ETC.

THE tribes which I am about to describe are doubtless not altogether unknown by report to various members of this Society, and I do not claim for myself the credit of bringing forward many new facts concerning them. My simple object is to promote attention to the subject in hopes of ultimately eliciting some more certain information than we possess as to the origin of races whose early history is shrouded in mystery and doubt.

All personal experiences, however slight, are of value as contributions to the general fund of information, and I have, therefore, not hesitated to comply with the request made to me, that I would communicate such particulars concerning the hill-tribes of the Nilgiris as came under my own observation during a three years' sojourn on those hills, otherwise known as the Blue Mountains of the Deccan.

It is not necessary here to describe that well-known range further than to observe, for better understanding the situation of the tribes by whom it is inhabited, that it occupies a nearly isolated position, has a superficial extent calculated at between six and seven hundred square miles, and an extreme central altitude of 8,760 feet. Approaching them through the flat parched district of Coimbatoor, the great abruptness with which these mountains rise from the plain adds to their apparent height, and at a distance of many miles the grandeur of the lofty blue line elicits the admiration of the traveller. Arrived at the stifling village of Metapollium, at their base, and near the forest entrance of the ascent by the Coonoor Pass, gazing upwards on their hanging forests, rhododendron-sprinkled heights, and precipitous grey crags, towering almost perpendicularly to a height of 7,000 feet, one may fancy oneself enjoying a glimpse of another world. Notwithstanding the temptation which its lofty verdant summits must have offered to Europeans dwelling on the burning plains below, this range remained, chiefly on account of the then almost impenetrable belt of jungle, abounding in tigers and elephants, and surrounding its base on every side, unexplored till the year 1819, and it was not till two years later that any road was opened up to the summit.

Strange and unknown tribes were then found in possession of this favoured region, a region of green hills and sheltered hollows, of sparkling streams and tracts of primeval forest, with abundant vegetation and delightful climate. Todas and Khotas occupied the higher ranges, while Erulas and Kurumbas clustered here and there in the lower belts on the mountain sides.

These tribes I shall notice in order. Before, however, proceeding to do so, I may render my account plainer by briefly noticing another people who are located on the same ground, and in constant intercourse with the more immediate subjects of our notice, viz., the Vadacas or Badaghas, commonly called Burghers.

Though generally classed among the hill-tribes, they have, comparatively speaking, but recently come among them, having migrated from the plains lying to the northward of the range, not much more than two hundred years ago. Their history is well known, and there is so little that is new or remarkable about them, that were it not for their intimate connection with the every-day life of the Todas and other hill-tribes, any detailed mention of them would be unnecessary. Although simply Hindoos, their original characteristics and dialect have naturally become somewhat modified in the course of the six or seven generations during which they have inhabited a locality so different to that from which they emigrated.

They are lighter in colour than the Hindoos proper, and also than any of the true hill-tribes, from whom they are besides easily distinguished at a distance on account of their wearing turbans. They are beardless, slightly built, and smooth in limb.

Several different classes exist among them, the more wealthy owning the only cows and oxen on the hills, as well as herds of buffaloes; many cultivate considerable tracts of grain and other agricultural produce; while the lowest grade either work for the others as labourers or hire themselves out to Europeans, being the only people on these hills who do so.

Their worship is that of Siva, and a separate caste among them, the Lingaits, are the priests. The Lingam is the combination of the male and female Phallic symbols of Siva and Parvati, but this religion is free from the impurities that accompany the usual forms of Hindoo Phallism, and is stern and severe. Every Vadaca village has its Lingam, which, if not actually worshipped by all, is held in universal reverence. The mass of the people appear to believe in Rangasawmie and other minor deities. These gods occupy thatched temples of sun-baked mud, and in front of each is a roughly-hewn flat stone or altar for the reception of the offerings of the devout.

I found in a solitary part of the hills near Hoolicul, half-hidden in lemon-grass nearly its own height, a temple of more interest, dedicated to Hetti. It consisted of two parts, the temple itself being a small thatched clay case like a large beehive, standing on a platform raised five or six feet from the ground. This contained, as I was told, portions of the clothing of a deceased Vadaca of wealth and of his widow, who had undergone the suttee with his corpse. Sutteeism, it may be observed, formerly prevailed among these people, even after their arrival on the hills, though now for some generations discontinued. Opposite to, and a few paces from, this small memorial temple stood half-a-dozen spear-headed stakes placed in two rows, and connected by an ornamented transverse bar, having a seventh point, and hung with grass cords. The sketch will convey a better idea of it. These simple erections, from their perishable nature, and from the custom which they commemorate, having become obsolete, are now rarely met with on the hills.

The Vadaca funeral rites are at the present day so far modified as regards the suttee that the widow merely pretends to rush towards the blazing pile to sacrifice herself with her husband's dead body, and is pulled back by her friends, who throw her robe on the funeral pyre instead, and she herself commences a new lease of life with new clothing.

The villages of the Vadacas very much resemble those of the Hindoos of the plains, and are more numerous and of greater size than any others on the hills, frequently containing from thirty to forty houses. The number of the tribe is computed to be between eight and nine thousand, or fifteen to one, as compared with the Todas.

All the Vadacas may be considered as feudal vassals of the latter, by whose permission they remained on their first arrival, in certain appointed districts, for the occupation of which they pay tribute in grain—a certain fixed percentage on their crops. They pay great deference to the Todas, and never pass them without salaaming. Being a most industrious agricultural people, they have largely increased in wealth, and are prosperous and thriving. They are, nevertheless, besides being totally illiterate, superstitious and timid to an extraordinary degree, and to this cause may in part be attributed their continued subjection to the mere handful of men which the Todas really are.

The Todas, though by no means the most numerous, are, from an anthropological point of view, the most important and most interesting, being, doubtless, also by far the most ancient of the tribes of the Nilgiris. To them, therefore, the greater part of my observations will be devoted.

Totally distinct in aspect, mould, and bearing from any of the various races of the low country, and as markedly different from the rest of the tribes immediately around them, their exceptional and striking appearance at once arrests the eye of the most unobservant.

The men are large in frame, tall and remarkably well-proportioned, with muscular, massive, and very hairy limbs and broad chests; a physique totally opposite in every respect to that of the dwellers in the plains. Their countenances are manly, open, and handsome, the features being unusually regular. They have luxuriant black beards, and, wearing no turban or covering on the head, display to full advantage their clustering bushy hair, the European look of which is increased by their practice of wearing it parted down the centre. In colour they are nearer brown than black; their lips are full rather than large, and their cheek-bones marked but not high. The eyes are large and intelligent, and the nose is elevated and arched. It is doubtless this combination of the distinguishing features of the white race, with an almost black complexion that gives them in part their peculiar aspect. Many of them have a very Jewish expression, but the general contour of the head and cast of countenance are rather such as we are accustomed to associate with the ancient Romans. This similitude is also enhanced by their stately carriage and flowing robe, the loose folds of which give them an appearance best described by the term classic. This garment, in which the Toda envelopes himself, is of a thick coarse cotton cloth of native manufacture, white when clean, and having a red stripe or border. It is hung over the left shoulder, brought across the back and forward under the right arm, the point being flung backwards over the left shoulder again, leaving the right arm at liberty, and allowing the folds to fall gracefully about the lower part of the person down to the knees. When herding their buffaloes, the men carry a thin straight rod or wand, about six feet in length, and this is the only approach to implement or weapon that they ever use.

The women are much lighter in hue than the men, the body being of a *café-au-lait* tint, and the face a shade darker. They are as a rule very pleasing in expression, and the young women, from fifteen to twenty, generally exceedingly good-looking. They are above the middle height, large in frame and well developed, though the hands and feet are very small. Their features are regular, the mouth not large, lips often thin, and the teeth even and beautifully white; the nose is straight, whilst the eyes are dark and expressive. The most striking peculiarity about them is the arrangement of their fine glossy black hair, which is dressed in ringlets precisely such as ladies in this country wore about twenty or five-and-twenty years ago. On the top of the head the hair is smoothed and parted with the greatest care, and the long ringlets hang on either side of the oval face with a neatness and regularity strangely at variance with their apparently rough mode of life; the hair in both sexes is anointed with ghee, as is also the skin. The female dress on ordinary occasions consists simply of a single robe similar to that of the men, though it is worn differently, being merely thrown over both shoulders and clasped in front by the hand. This, as one very soon learns, generally constitutes the sole garment of the wearer, for the Toda women have a habit, even in the presence of strangers, of throwing open the mantle to the full extent of both arms for the purpose of readjusting it on the shoulders. Some of them indeed hardly take the trouble to hold it together in front at all, and this was especially the case at a *mund*, near Coonoor, which, as I was quartered in the immediate vicinity, I had frequently to pass. I used to notice that the men watching their herds on the opposite heights, separated by a wide glen from where I was, would announce my coming by shouting across to the women at home, who were accordingly always on the *qui vive* at the roadside prepared to greet me with their usual begging cry *Enam Kurroo*, "give me a present." The way that these men carry on conversations with one another across wide intervening valleys, and apparently without effort, reminded me of the Kaffir herdsmen, every word of whose voices I have heard from hill-tops at distances that seemed incredible.

I have on occasions of ceremony seen the women with underclothing fastened round the middle in addition to the above everyday costume. I may observe that they often embroider the corners of these robes with blue thread, and shew very considerable taste in the devices.

Neither slippers nor sandals are ever seen among them, men, women, and children alike, going barefooted. The young children are generally pleasing in their appearance. I noticed that the boys up to eight or ten years old are of the same light colour as the girls, the dark hue of later life being gradually developed with each year's exposure to the sun and mountain air until the age of manhood. It is to be noted, however, of the females that, though equally exposed to climatic influences, their complexions remain nearly the same all through life.

The lineaments and characteristics of the Telingan race, as described by Pickering, seem to apply to this people in all points save one, but that a very important one, namely, the nature of the hair. According to the above author, the Telingans have "straight fine hair", but, as the hair of the Toda men is clustering, partially curled, and rather inclined to coarseness, the classification of this tribe under that head seems out of the question.

The most noticeable of the ornaments, generally valuable and always pleasing to the eye, worn by the Toda women, are their massive and very handsome necklaces of solid gold and silver, which, though of course varying in size and detail of design, are all of the same typical character, resembling some of the ancient necklaces found in our own country. These ornaments they value very highly, and regard as heirlooms not to be parted with on any consideration, so that to procure a specimen was a matter of extreme difficulty. The one now exhibited I managed after much trouble to obtain through the medium of a friendly Moravian missionary, from a female whose interest in dress and ornament was, like herself, somewhat on the wane. Mr. Metz, the missionary in question, in the course of a residence of many years among these people, had gained their trust and confidence to an almost unlimited extent; nevertheless, it required, in addition to his oral arguments, several successive handfuls of small silver coin, finally amounting to thirty-five rupees to induce her to sell it. Even this sum (which was about equivalent to £3 : 10 : 0, in shillings and sixpences) the owner consented to accept only on condition that nothing should be said to any of her tribe regarding the transaction. This ornament is the work of the Khotas, one of the tribes that will be presently described, and its weight is nearly eight ounces of the purest silver. Nearly all the adult women have similar necklaces, many of them being much larger and more massive than the present specimen, and mostly having bunches and rosettes of cowrie shells on blue cords affixed, which hang down the back of the neck.

Their other ornaments are silver ear-rings and bracelets; gold, silver, and brass rings on the fingers, a couple of very large brass armlets above the elbows, and a brass or sometimes silver belt worn round the middle, and next to the skin. The use of the latter I fancy may be the suspension of the underclothing when worn.

The dwelling of the Toda, though in no way very remarkable, differs, nevertheless, from that of any other uncivilised people that I have met with. The walls are made of roughly planed boards joined with clay; the sides are not more than three feet high, by about twelve feet long, and the ends are gables about eight feet high, having slightly rounded points. The roof is made of reeds, and thatched with lemon-grass, a tall and very strong plant attaining a height of six to eight feet, having a strong perfume of lemon, and growing luxuriantly on the hills.

The whole structure is very substantially and neatly built, but

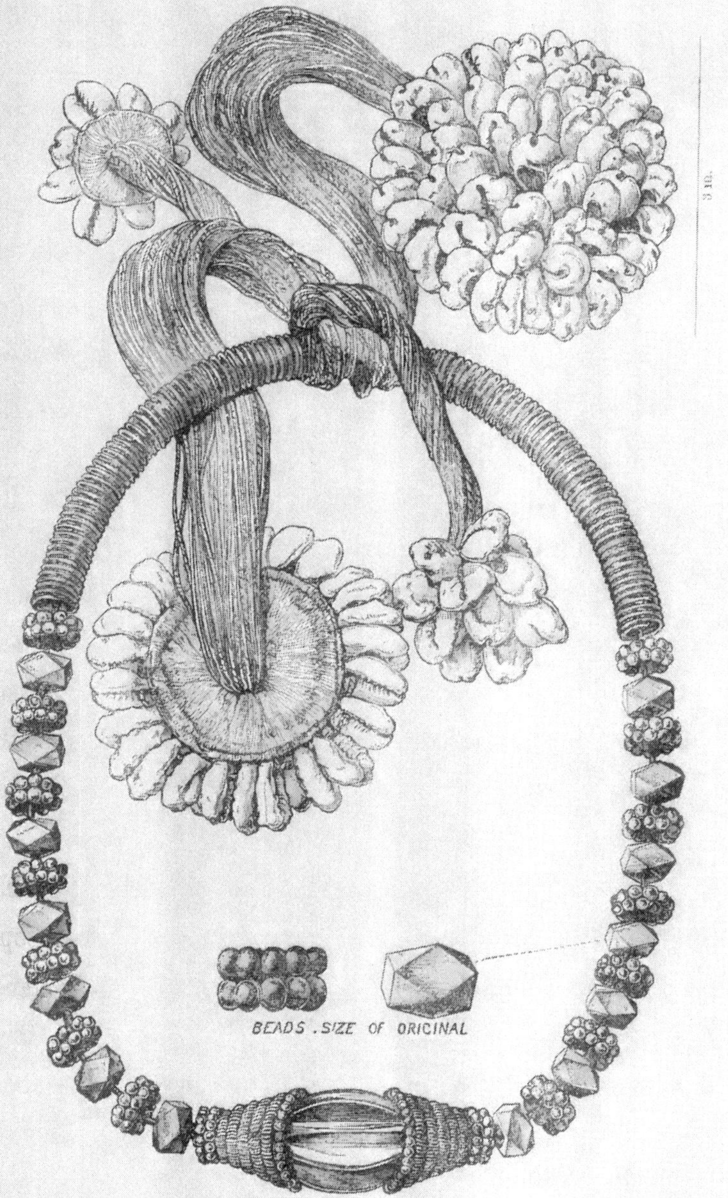

SILVER NECKLACE, TODA TRIBE.

there is no chimney, and the smoke from the fires pours out at the door and exudes from every crevice. The entrance is an opening just sufficient to admit a full-grown person on hands and knees, and is made to close from within. There is in front of the dwellings, partly enclosed by a low wall of loose stones, an open grassy space or court, which, owing to the nomadic habits of the Todas, is always of a fresh green. The huts are built close together on some naturally smooth knoll in clusters of three or four only, and not in villages; these family groups are called *munds.*

There is always one hut set apart for the reception of milk, and this is placed a little to one side of the other huts, which in construction it precisely resembles. It is entirely surrounded by a low wall, within which no females are permitted to enter on any account, nor are they allowed even to milk the buffaloes; a custom or rule which I have found existing also among the Kaffirs of South Africa.

The *munds* are situated at considerable distances apart, and their inhabitants migrate periodically from one to another for change of pasture. During the dry season—that is, from the beginning of January to the end of April—they are in the habit of setting fire to the grass, with a view to promoting its better growth; another Kaffir custom, and one, moreover, the beautiful effect of which at night will be remembered by all who have ever seen it on so large a scale.

Before leaving, the Todas close the entrances to their dwellings, but take no further care regarding them. I found several times in the course of the three years that I spent on these hills, various *munds* suddenly deserted, and again, after an interval of some two or three months, as suddenly reoccupied. As there was nothing to prevent any curious person from entering these empty huts, I took the liberty of doing so in one or two instances, but always found them totally destitute of either utensils or furniture, and even of fixtures, beyond a raised earthen ledge along the foot of the wall, answering the purpose of a table. They were all without any light, beyond that which could find an entrance through the aperture which does duty as a door.

The total strength of the Todas at the present day is probably under eight hundred, of all ages. It is impossible to form an estimate of the original importance and numbers of such a people; but there are indications of former Toda *munds* where none now exist, so that the tribe has doubtless been more numerous at some past epoch.

It is the boast of the Todas that they are hereditary and original lords of the soil, and owners of the whole of the Nilgiris, a claim fully allowed by the other tribes, as evidenced by their paying tribute for the land, and owning a sort of feudal vassalage. Each Toda family has its own territorial property, or district, and the Vadacas living on it are, as already stated, simply tenants, paying an annual tax, or rent in kind, for the land they live on or cultivate. We also, I believe, acknowledge their title by paying a yearly tax for our occupation. The natural peacefulness of the Toda tribe, together with their ignorance of war, make it improbable that their ancestors ever forcibly usurped the territory, and they have doubtless always been regarded by the other tribes as a superior race, entitled to it from immemorial possession and residence.

Their language affords no clue to their origin, and is as strange and peculiar as themselves. It is deep-toned, harsh, and difficult of pronunciation, and without written character. It is neither spoken nor understood by the other hill-tribes with whom they are in almost daily contact, though one would have imagined that the necessity for communication for purposes of barter or exchange would, in course of time, have caused a mutual knowledge of their languages; but it is the Todas only who have acquired the means of communication, having just so much knowledge of the speech of their vassals as is demanded by the most ordinary requirements. The Toda tongue is said to comprise words of Sanskrit and Tamul origin, and to have a certain limited similarity in grammatical structure to the latter language. In all other respects, it differs widely from it or any known tongue either of the vast Indian empire, or of any other country. Recent research has disproved the formerly accepted theory that the languages of Southern India, viz., Telinga, Carnataca, Tamul, and Malayalim, were corrupt derivatives of Sanskrit, and it is believed that the few Sanskrit words which occur in the Toda tongue have merely been engrafted on it.

With reference to the Tamul, a partial similarity, or even identity, in the vocabulary of any language might arise simply from lengthened local proximity, and is only considered by philologists as of any value when it occurs in what are supposed to be the most ancient words; namely, those which pertain to every-day life, such as no nation, even its most primitive state, could be without, and which would be the least likely to be exchanged for foreign words. As to the resemblance in grammatical construction, which is said to consist in some plurals and in the terminations of certain verbs, an oral language so difficult of pronunciation will naturally demand a great amount of careful study and an intimate acquaintance, in order to determine with certainty the value of this affinity. Moreover, supposing it to be established, it appears to be a question whether the Tamul might not owe its root to the aboriginal Toda, instead of *vice versa*.

In mental constitution the Toda is intelligent and thoughtful; although naturally indolent, capable of being roused to considerable exertion on occasions of necessity; and, notwithstanding his singularly peaceful disposition, and total want of weapons, is inherently brave and bold. It has been said that he is too lazy to hunt the wild game, large or small, which abounds on every side; but it must be remembered that he does not eat flesh. Possessing no implements of agriculture, he consequently does not till the ground, but the grain which he uses is supplied by his vassals as a *quid pro quo*, in which respect he differs little from the wealthy classes in more civilised countries. The very use of grain at all by the Todas is probably an innovation of recent date. That physical courage is not wanting in an average Toda may be inferred from the bloody funeral customs which, as will be presently described, prevail in his country. His moral fearlessness of character, with its accompanying consciousness of power, are felt and acknowledged by all the other tribes, who involuntarily bow to an influence they can neither cope with nor emulate. His contempt of danger is also exhibited in his carrying no weapon of defence against the numerous cheetahs, black panthers, bears, wild dogs, and tigers which haunt the hills, although the latter, as I can testify, frequently attack and kill his buffaloes. During my sojourn out there, parties of Todas would often come many miles distance to give us information of these occurrences, both for the sake of the *enam*, or present, they got for so doing, as well as to obtain the assistance of a rifle or two, to rid them of their enemy. The practice on these occasions is to repair to the spot where the carcase of the partly eaten buffalo has been left, and to lie in wait till dark for the tiger, which invariably returns at night to feast on his prey. To show the activity and endurance of these men, I may mention that I have seen them at such times, after having walked ten or twelve miles in the heat of the sun, stand talking to one another till our horses were ready, and then, without any sort of refreshment or rest whatever, set out on their return with the greatest alacrity, keeping up with us the whole way.

The buffaloes in question are of the kind one sees in Egypt and on the plains of India, black-skinned, ungainly animals, sparsely sprinkled with long coarse bristles, and having wide-spreading flattened horns. The herds belonging to the Todas comprise, however, very much larger and finer animals than are to be found in the low country; they are, moreover, exceedingly savage when Europeans come near them. I have frequently been charged by a whole herd when on horseback, and obliged to take to a smart canter to avoid them. Nevertheless, one may see them any day driven at will by little naked Toda urchins. Each *mund* has an enclosure or pen called a *tooel*, in which the buffaloes are confined at night; it is generally circular in form, and consists of a low wall of loose stones surrounding a sunk area within. As these pens are never cleaned out, the interior becomes in time so much elevated, that the fence has to be heightened by the addition of thorns and cut branches. When the buffaloes come home at evening, the Todas who may be standing near invariably salute them with the greatest gravity and respect. Though they have numerous large herds of these animals, the Todas never kill them for food, keeping them solely for the sake of their milk. There are a certain number of sacred buffaloes belonging to each of their *Terrarees*, or holy places, and these are never milked, but with their young by their sides, lead a privileged life, the honour being apparently hereditary. Milk is, it may be mentioned, the principal diet of these people, either in its natural state, or sour, like that used by the natives of South Africa. All vegetable food, except the wild fruits which they gather themselves, such as yellow blackberries, wild plums, the hill-gooseberry,* or cherry, as some call it, is obtained from the Vadacas, as already explained. This consists generally of green pulse, barley, millet, and other seeds, which it is the women's duty to winnow and grind, performing the latter operation between two roughly formed circular stones,

---

* *Physalis edulis*, a plant about twelve to eighteen inches high, bearing bladder-like pods, enclosing a round yellow fruit, about the size of a common gooseberry, of a very agreeable subacid flavour.

the lower one fixed, and the upper revolving on it, similar to the ancient querns of Great Britain. It is singular that, though so attached to their buffaloes, the Todas keep no other domestic animal, not even the ubiquitous dog, the companion of man in every quarter of the globe from the polar regions to the equator. I never once saw or heard of a dog in any of their *munds*. This peculiarity, by the way, was specially remarked as a distinguishing trait in the history of the people of the European Drift period; and the dislike, and even abhorrence, evinced towards that animal by the ancient Jews is well known.

I should have mentioned that the Toda tribe is divided into two classes—the sacred, and what may be called for want of a better term the lay. The latter and more numerous class are called *Khootas*, whilst the former are known as the *Terrallees*. These appear to stand in regard to the rest of the community somewhat as did the Levites of old to the children of Israel, as it is from among them alone that the priests can be elected. No marriage can by Toda law take place between these two classes, though it is now sometimes evaded, and the breach winked at. Moreover, a priest, so long as he holds that office, cannot marry, and must keep aloof from all others, excepting those who, like himself, are invested with the sacred character. In order to qualify for this, however, he has to undergo certain initiatory ceremonies and trials, such as long fasting, sleeping in the forest, naked and alone, for several nights in succession; the danger from wild beasts, and the endurance of the chill night-air of these elevated regions, being deemed sufficiently severe tests of his fitness for the office. When fully appointed, the chief priests are distinguished by a different dress from their *confrères*. The subordinate priests, or coadjutors, whose native title, like the others, I cannot recal, undergo a shorter and less severe period of initiation. Both are often dairymen, an office of great honour and importance; but a *Khoota* is equally eligible, provided he goes through certain preparatory rites in order to purify himself for it. The especial duties of the priests are to tend the sacred herds just mentioned; to conduct the periodical sacrifice of a calf to invoke fruitfulness among their herds; to present the daily offering of milk at their temples; and to superintend the funeral rites. Of actual or of assembled worship, they have none, so far as I could discover, though, individually, they offer up occasional prayers to an Invisible Being for recovery or preservation from sickness.

Their temples differ but little in appearance from the ordinary huts. One of them, standing in a pretty little glen, near the road between Jakatalla and Coonoor, I made an examination of at a time when the *mund*, about half a mile off, to which it belonged was deserted by its inhabitants. Creeping in on all fours, I discovered, as well as the darkness permitted, that it contained nothing whatever but a square metal bell and a shapeless black stone, about twice the size of a man's head, the latter placed alone on the floor at the end furthest from the entrance. Being unwilling to bring this out to the light, I could not ascertain whether its colour was natural or artificial. The size precluded the notion of its being an aerolite, although it is well known that meteoric stones have been, in the early history of many countries, regarded with religious awe. To this temple, I had often previously seen the priest from the neighbouring *mund* bring, in the early morning, a vessel of new milk; but whether the offering was poured out, as some say it is, as a libation, or merely presented and taken away again, I had no means of ascertaining without the risk of giving annoyance.

It will be borne in mind that black stones have, from the earliest times, been objects of reverence or actual adoration from east to west; as, for instance, in Mecca, also among the ancient Romans, and even in the western islands of Scotland, where, moreover, milk was offered to them. Bells, too, have been, in past ages, regarded with veneration, and as having mysterious powers over demons and evil spirits, not only by various Eastern races and castes, but in ancient Britain.

The Todas believe in the existence of an invisible and supreme Spirit, and in a future state, though this they seem to regard as one of a somewhat mundane character, inasmuch as buffaloes and abundance of milk are to be the portion of the faithful. They also pay reverence to, though they do not worship, inferior objects, such as hills and forests and the rising sun, precisely as did the ancient Celts. In connection with the adoration of light, they also make an obeisance to their evening lamps on lighting them. The observance of this custom in Europe is mentioned by Edward Spencer, who, writing in 1596' states that, "at the kindling of fire and lighting of candles, the Scots and Irish use superstitious rites."*

---

* *Early Races of Scotland.*

The presence in their temples of large stones, which have, by superficial observers, been regarded as gods, has led to the belief that these people are idolaters; but this is certainly not the case. There is no doubt that the shapeless symbols are merely representatives of an unseen power, and not in themselves actual objects of worship; though with other races, preserving less strictly their primitive character, this original use has degenerated into idolatry. The fact, therefore, that this tribe has so preserved to the present day, in the midst of a heathen country, the primary object and intention of such symbols, is one worthy of notice; and leads to the supposition that the Todas may be equally unchanged in all other respects since the earliest days of their corporate existence as a people.

It would be a most interesting point to determine satisfactorily whether or not the early progenitors of the Todas were the erectors of the numerous Druidical circles and remains found on their hills, and which crown the summit of almost every peak throughout the Nilgiri range. Several of the cromlechs have, rather against the wishes of the hill-tribes, been examined at different times, and found to contain urns of clay filled with black earth, charred fragments of human bones, and roughly made clay figures of buffaloes, and in some instances bells; the whole lying under large flat stones within the circle. It is to be noted, too, that these urns, as well as the bells, very closely resemble those that have been found in Great Britain.

Within the last few months, "a set of iron implements" has

been found in a cromlech on the southern side of the Nilgiri range. The description given of them is as yet so vague that it is impossible to judge of their exact character; but I believe that they resemble the bill-hook and sword or dagger form.

I found cairns and other remains in the straths running up between the higher summits—on which, as before stated, they are more usually found—as stone altars, surrounded by a ring of smaller stones, and mounds of earth enclosed by circular walls.

The circles are evidently regarded with veneration by the Todas, as well as by the Vadacas; but it is difficult to elicit information concerning them. Though the former tribe neither use sepulchral urns nor erect monuments at the present day, they invariably burn the remains of their dead within a circle of stones, and afterwards bury them there, as will be hereafter described; while the presence of the buffalo images, and the similarity in make and texture of the ancient urns to the modern pottery of their workpeople, the Khotas, seem to indicate some connection between the Todas of past days and the remains in question.

The Todas are especially remarkable for the practice of polyandry, a custom which exists among but few tribes, as, for instance, in parts of Thibet and of the Himalayas, among the Nayrs of Malabar, and one or two other races only. A Toda woman often has three or four husbands, who are all brothers, and with each of whom she cohabits a month at a time. What is more singular, such young men as, by the paucity of women among the tribe, are prevented from obtaining a share in a wife, are allowed, with the permission of the fraternal husbands, to become temporary partners with them.

Notwithstanding these singular family arrangements, the greatest harmony appears to prevail among all parties—husbands, wives, and lovers. The children live happily with their putative parents, equally well treated on every side, and as common to all alike, though, I believe, if any special reason demands it, the senior husband can claim the elder children.

The betrothal to the first husband commences at a very early age; and all subsequent brothers of the bridegroom elect become from their birth bound to the common prospective wife. The compact, as regards the first pair, is conducted by their respective male parents; the father of the bridegroom *in esse* presenting a buffalo and a new robe to the other, the acceptance of which is understood to ratify the agreement. When, in due course of time, the marriage takes place, the bride, who is probably about fifteen or sixteen years of age, receives from her father a dowry of several buffaloes, together with necklaces, armlets, and ear-rings. The ceremony is generally celebrated by a dance, which, though not of a very exciting description, seems to afford sufficient satisfaction to these cheerful, good-natured people. It consists of stamping on each foot alternately, the body being jerked half round at one step, and back again at the next, to the time of a very monotonous song.

When about to become a mother, in place of receiving every comfort and consideration, the Toda woman is sent out, or, what amounts to the same thing, is by custom expected to go out into the forest, and there remain alone, protected only in case of stormy weather by the shelter of the bushes. After the child is born, it is not allowed to be seen by anyone but its parents for some weeks, at the end of which time it is duly named and presented in public.

It is a fact worth noticing that, notwithstanding the scarcity of women (said to be owing to the practice of female infanticide which prevailed till within a very few years ago), the Todas never contract marriages with the other tribes, though living together on most friendly terms. That there never has been any mixture of the races, is sufficiently evident from the strongly marked distinctions that continue to exist between them.

It is not less singular, on the other hand, that, in spite of the system of intermarriage which has thus prevailed among the Todas for many generations, or it may be ages, there should not only be no sign of physical deterioration, but that both sexes should be so remarkable for their stature, pleasing exterior, and noble bearing. This would seem to confirm the theory that the marriage of relations, however closely connected, would, in cases of mutual faultless constitution and physical form, result in these excellences of the parents being transmitted, just as in the opposite case physical and mental defects common to both are transmitted, and even augmented.

When a death occurs among the Todas, the corpse, covered over with certain aromatic herbs, is left in the hut either till distant friends are summoned, or until the occurrence of a propitious day for the burial; these people being firm believers in lucky and unlucky days. Each night and morning of the interval between the death and the funeral, a lament or coronach is sung over the body by the family and relatives of the deceased. In this they are often joined by passing friends, or by those who have come for the purpose of thus testifying their respect for the dead, and sympathy with the survivors—a trait in the character of this people exhibited in many other ways, and more remarkably than with even many civilised nations.

The day of a death is observed by the immediate relatives, as it was among the ancient Jews, as a solemn fast. Their necklaces and ear-rings are also taken off, and the hair is cut short, as a sign of grief and mourning. Both sexes are obliged to conform to this custom on the death of a near male relation, though when a female dies the men do not do so. The sacred class, or *Terralees*, are exempt in either case.

On an appointed day, the relatives from a distance having duly arrived in obedience to the summons, the body covered over with a mantle, but having the face exposed, is carried in procession on a sort of bier to the *Terraree*, or sacred ground belonging to the family, and, under the superintendence of the high priest attached thereto, assisted by his subordinate, is burned with certain solemnities and much wailing; the relatives, prior to the corpse being placed on the funeral pile, cutting off a few locks from the head.

The above are, however, only the preliminary honours paid to the dead, the principal rites being deferred to a subsequent period, which may be a few weeks, or as many months later.

With a view to the coming rites, portions of the deceased's ashes are saved from the pyre, and, together with the locks of hair, his ear-rings and other ornaments, are carefully folded in his own mantle, and laid by until the proper time arrives.

The concluding ceremonies are, perhaps, the most singular and interesting of all the Toda customs, and I was fortunate in having an unusually favourable opportunity of witnessing them. For, familiar as some of their practices have latterly become in the neighbourhood of our new Hill-stations, their funeral obsequies are only celebrated in the more remote parts of the mountains, and are consequently seldom seen by any European. Indeed, I do not know that the presence of Captain J. and myself would have been tolerated on the occasion to which I refer, had we not been accompanied, or rather introduced, by the Moravian missionary, Mr. Metz, whom I have already mentioned as being so much esteemed by the tribe.

Our ride to Kapilla, the scene of these interesting rites, lay for some miles over a fine open undulating table-land dotted with enormous rhododendrons, which were loaded with clusters of dark crimson flowers. Gradually we got into higher ground, now pressing our hill-ponies up steep acclivities, now skirting the edge of great forest belts stretching downwards for many a mile into the sultry valleys at our feet, till, guided by the appearance of a few distant natives wending their way towards an isolated wood on one of the surrounding mist-covered peaks, we at length came within hearing of the shrill and very peculiar sound of Khota hautboys.

Leaving our ponies, we entered a deep shadowy wood of moss-grown trees, whose gnarled and twisted stems and branches were also completely covered overhead and down to the ground with ferns, orchids, long pendent tufts of grey lichen, and parasitical plants, one with dark glossy leaves and an orange flower being especially beautiful.

In an open space, near the centre of this shady grove, and lit up by the bright rays of the midday sun, was a surging crowd of white-robed Todas, and half-naked Khotas with wild and excited looks, whose unmusical pipes drowned all other sounds. Outside the wood, on an open green space, stood a Toda temple, having its gable-ends of polished wood thickly studded over with silver coins of various sizes, fixed in perpendicular rows on each alternate plank. Near at hand was a small temporary shed, or ridge-shaped tent, made of pieces of native cloth, whilst at a little distance off was a large circular *tooel*, or cattle kraal, with a wall both higher and thicker and altogether much more substantial than usual. It was constructed of stones and sun-baked clay, the entrance being barred with stout poles.

Within this enclosure stood ten splendid buffaloes, their clean bright skins and polished horns indicating that some pains had been taken to improve their naturally fine appearance.

Crowds of women and children stood or sat about the temple, in which a party of the former had just placed the deceased's robe and ornaments, together with two bags containing his ashes. With the exception of the younger children, who were naked, the whole were clad in clean, white, soft-looking mantles, and wore ear-rings and necklaces of gold and silver. A plaintive monotonous wail was sustained while each man arriving passed before and bowed towards the dead man's ashes.

All the males, except one or two grey-headed old patriarchs who sat with great dignity a little aside, now danced together in a circle holding hands, the Khota musicians accompanying them with tom-toms and pipes.

When this was concluded half-a-dozen young men, evidently selected for their strength and activity, came forward, each carrying a long heavy club made of dark wood and pointed at the thicker end. Having thrown off the usual mantle, they stood in a kind of kilt of thick white cloth, having a red border round the lower edge, or skirt, the upper part of their bodies, as well as the legs, being bare. In this picturesque and most becoming costume they looked exceedingly handsome fellows, models as they were of muscular symmetry. At once advancing towards the cattle enclosure, with all the women and children running after them in the greatest excitement, these combatants leaped in among the buffaloes, the crowd instantly closing round and completely covering the wall, each endeavouring to get as good a view as possible of the coming spectacle.

The buffaloes were, as may be supposed, alarmed by these unusual proceedings, and their alarm became all the greater when the clubmen dancing wildly in their midst commenced striking them with their clubs. When their panic was at its height the men, watching their opportunity, sprang two together on the necks of three of the largest animals simultaneously, seizing them by the horns and nostrils and endeavouring to bear them to the ground, and affix a collar and bell round their necks. This bell is of the kind usually worn by one or more animals in every herd when grazing, and is of the ancient four-sided form, made of a single plate of metal and roughly riveted.

Marvellous was the agility displayed by these gladiators, as we may term them, in avoiding the savage thrusts of the huge sharp-pointed horns and in getting in behind them on to the animal's neck, wrestling in desperate strife as they were borne here and there among the trampling feet, now dashed against the wall, now on the ground.

To escape unhurt in such a combat was impossible, and it was not long before we saw one of the men receive a dangerous wound in the neck from the thrust of a horn, which ripped open a wide gash from the collar-bone to the ear. He at once became an object of the greatest solicitude among the women, and was led away as a hero to the small tent, where he received every care and attention at their gentle hands.

As, one after another, fresh animals were attacked and borne to the ground with terrific struggles, those already belled and liberated turned on the common enemy, angrily tossing their formidable horns and butting so savagely that, had it not been for the extreme quickness and coolness of these men, some of them must have been killed. Their clubs now swung round and aloft with greater rapidity, and the heavy blows fell thicker and faster, the loud shouts and excited gestures of the male spectators, the exulting *Hau, hau* of the combatants, the terror and occasional shrieks of the women, the stamping and rushing in the arena, the bellowing of the buffaloes, whose nostrils were covered with blood and foam, and the circling clouds of dust half hiding the writhing mass, formed a whole more easily pictured in the mind than in words. A bag of the deceased's ashes was now laid at the entrance to the kraal, and the high priest, taking a handful or two of earth, threw some of it on the ashes, and some into the kraal amongst the buffaloes. One of these lay dead in the enclosure, and the rest were one by one led, or rather dragged out to their final doom, struggling violently, and plunging right and left in vain endeavours to escape from their brawny captors, who again clung to their necks. Forced up to a post fixed in the ground, at the foot of which lay the robe, ornaments, and ashes brought from the temple, the battered, bleeding animals were at length despatched there by the high priest's sacrificial axe as an offering to the dead.

Though the women had beheld with interest and excitement the torture of these unfortunate brutes, they now exhibited the greatest grief at their death, sitting and kneeling round the carcases with clasped hands and streaming eyes, addressing them in the most affectionate terms, as "Are you happy?" "Is it well with you?"

The mourners, male and female, next drew near to each other in couples, the man putting out first the right foot and then the left towards the woman he approached, who, dropping on one knee, touched it with her forehead. Both parties then seated themselves on the ground close to and facing each other, and bringing their foreheads together remained in that attitude, with their hands placed either on each other's knees or shoulders, the woman weeping aloud, and having her mantle drawn closely over the head. In a few minutes the man would rise, and with a plaintive ejaculation, go to another to perform again the same ceremony, invariably offering first his foot, which was always saluted with the forehead.

All this weeping and wailing, divided as it was between the buffaloes and the dead man, had a most striking effect. So unfeigned did their grief appear that I could not but feel that our presence was an intrusion. This scene continued until the mourners, who formed only a portion of those present, had all gone through the ceremony one with the other, when the priest, standing by the deceased's ashes and robe, laid on them a handful of what appeared to me, as far as I could see, to be some kind of seed or grain, and then, accompanied by the under priest, bore it back again with great reverence to the temple, the crowd falling back to permit the passage of the priests and their charge.

With this seemed to terminate the first part of the obsequies, and a sudden change came over the whole scene. The dead buffaloes were removed by noisy parties of Khotas, who had either bought them, or earned them by their services just concluded; and the crowd of Todas again assumed their every-day deportment, as they prepared for a general meal or feast.

We found that the rites would not be resumed till dark, when the robe and ornaments were to be burned; but, as we had no shelter to go to for the intervening seven hours, and no food for either ourselves or our ponies, which were, moreover, shivering from the cold of this elevated position, we were obliged to forego the gratification of witnessing the conclusion, but were shown the spot where it was to take place. This was within a circle of stones, exhibiting signs of many former burnings, and occupying a retired situation at the edge of the grove.

In the centre of this ring, on a pile of dry wood, the priests place the mantle, bags of ashes, ornaments, and wand of the deceased, together with gourds and grass baskets of grain, for his sustenance in the other world, and the whole are ignited as the mourners stand round, the women with their heads still covered by the mantle, and the men joining in a monotonous cry of *heh-hey, heh-hah.* Every vestige of the remains is on this occasion destroyed by fire, and the metal ornaments having been carefully searched for, the ashes are buried under a large flat stone in the centre of the circle. This done, the ornaments are taken home by the family with every sign of respect and affection for the lost one.

The Khotas.—Next to the Todas in point of interest, and probably also in antiquity of race, as well as of settlement on the Hills, stand the Khotas, though the two races have nothing in common either as regards physical development, countenance, usages, or dwellings.

A party of Khotas seated, as I have often seen them, in the evening, outside their dingy huts, presents an exceedingly wild and weird appearance. Thin and spare in form, and very black, the men wear only a dirty cloth round the loins, and the uncomely women the common wrapper of the country. The bare heads of both sexes are shaggy, with matted locks of dusty hair, sometimes tied in a knot behind, and invariably uncombed from the day of their birth. This hair is different in nature from that of the Toda, and could it by any possibility be disentangled would be found naturally long and straight, instead of curly and clustering; the bushy beard is also absent, and every feature is of an opposite character to those of the tribe with which they are so closely in contact; the countenance being entirely destitute of that intelligent and pleasing expression so noticeable in the other.

Dirty in their dwellings and persons, they are also unclean feeders, devouring dead cattle, putrid flesh, birds of prey, or vermin, with as much apparent relish as fresh buffalo-meat, for which, unlike the Todas, they have a great predilection. I have myself seen a Khota carry home for food a dead rat thrown out of the stable a day or two previously by my *ghorawallah*. Practising such habits, it is not to be wondered at that the Todas consider them an unclean people.

On the other hand, they are a peaceful and industrious race, ingenious artisans, and indispensable to the other tribes, for whom they manufacture gold and silver ornaments, pottery, agricultural implements, wood-work, and baskets, besides acting, as already described, in the capacity of musicians at the funeral and other ceremonies of their less skilled neighbours. For these varied services they receive payment from the Todas in coin or buffaloes, and from the Vadacas in grain and other produce. It is to be observed though, that they do not, like the latter, hire themselves out as labourers, but preserve a certain independence, entirely confining their mechanical labours to the supply of their own wants and those of these two tribes; I never saw a Khota labouring either for a European, or on the public works, which at Jakatalla gave employment to so many of the neighbouring Vadacas.

Though their pottery (made exclusively by the women) is of a coarse and inferior quality, many of their gold and silver ornaments are, as will be seen by an examination of the necklace before noticed, artistic in conception, and exceedingly well executed. Its solid beads on either side are alternate polygonal cubes, and double rings of pellets, and are evidently cast in a mould; the centre ornament is an oval of more elaborate design, and is of beaten silver. One of their chief musical instruments is the pipe, also before mentioned as being used at the Toda funerals, and of this I managed to obtain the specimen exhibited. It is a sort of hautboy, being played by means of a reed, and having a bell-mouth, which is remarkably well made out of a solid piece of hard wood. I cannot, however, say much in favour of the musical properties of this instrument, the tones of which are loud and harsh, and bear an inferior resemblance to those of the Highland bagpipes.

It is probable that the Khotas have been as long resident on the Hills as the Todas, to whom they were doubtless originally, as at the present time, inferior, both physically and in general condition. Their ability as artisans is as much the result of manual dexterity as of intelligence, in which they are by no means superior to the Todas.

As there were in the days of Adam, pastoral tribes and mechanical ("such as have cattle," as well as "artificers in brass and iron"), each following their own special occupation, so these two tribes may have held their present position with regard to one another through successive ages to the present time.

The Khota tongue is said, by those who have examined it critically, to be in its root and origin allied to that of the Todas, though, as far as mere sound goes, which is the only experience of it that I possess, they are very unlike; nor do the two tribes understand one another.

In place of the deep pectoral and sonorous tones of the Toda, who always speaks with dignity and deliberation, the Khota has a rapid utterance with a somewhat nasal twang. The similarity that really exists in the formation of some words is, however, worthy of careful notice.

Though occupied chiefly as artisans, the Khotas, like their neighbours, keep up herds of buffaloes, and moreover, cultivate the ground to some extent, producing fair crops of grain, millet, garlic, mustard, poppy, pulse of several kinds, and what at first much surprised me, of our well-known garden flower called "prince's-feather."* The mustard is not used by them as far as I could learn, but is grown as an article of exchange, or barter with the low-country people; but the poppy is largely consumed among themselves, in the form of opium. Each family has a larger or smaller patch of land, not generally close to its dwelling, but in any suitable spot on the neighbouring verdant slopes. The

---

* *Amaranthus tristis.*

effect thus produced is often very beautiful: at one season sheets of scarlet poppy set in green, at another, of yellow-flowered mustard, alternating with brilliant ridges of crimson amaranthus, suggest rather the idea of ornamental "ribbon border" gardens of native design than practical farming. The prince's-feather is grown for its seed, which is called *keerie*; mixed with the flour of other grain, it is much used as food in the shape of porridge.

As is very generally the case among uncivilised tribes, a great proportion of the field work is performed by the women, whose, in this instance, not very pleasing form and features are by no means improved thereby. In addition to daily household duties, it is also their business to thrash out and winnow the grain, which latter operation they perform just outside their huts seated on a clean grass mat. Raising the corn or seed in baskets to the full upward extent of the arms, they pour it out so that the wind shall carry the chaff to one side. Afterwards the grain is parched a light brown colour, and finally ground between two stones, the meal being most ordinarily used in the form of porridge, as above stated. Every hut has in front a threshing-floor made of sun-baked and evenly smoothed clay, and this is also a favourite place of resort in the evening.

Though, like the Todas, they have numerous buffaloes, these keep them for an entirely opposite purpose; for, whereas the others feed them solely for the sake of their milk, and never use them for food, the Khotas do not milk them at all, but kill them as required, for the sake of their flesh only. It has been stated that they make no use whatever of their buffaloes, neither slaughtering them nor milking them, but this is an error. They use a good deal of the meat, more or less fresh, and are also in the habit of drying strips of it in the sun for future use, like the *biltong* of the South Africans.

The Khotas number at the present time probably about two thousand souls. One of their largest villages is that at Khotagiri, close to which I took up my abode for several weeks, on two different occasions. Though, as has been seen, the Toda *munds* never comprise more than four or five huts, the Khota villages cover some extent of ground, and the dwellings are of a totally different character to the others, in form as well as material. These are simply rough square-built cabins, with ridge roofs, thatched with grass, the walls being a mixture of clay and buffalo dung plastered over a framework of wattle and posts.

In each village are separate temples for the men and women, the larger, intended for the male sex, being dedicated to an imaginary deity, and the other to an equally mythological goddess. These temples, if they can be so called, are built similarly to the huts, except that they have the upper part of the gable-ends open, and the chief temple, which is double the size of an ordinary dwelling, is distinguished by several tall poles projecting above the ridge, and having feathers and bits of cloth attached and fluttering in the breeze. I was freely allowed to enter the large temple at Khotagiri, but found it a mere empty shed, no stones or symbols of any kind being visible. This confirmed what I had previously heard, namely, that the religion of these people does not partake of idolatry in any degree whatever, all their deities, of which there are several of both sexes, being purely ideal.

They have no separate sacred class like the Todas, though each village appears to have a family claiming an hereditary right to the priesthood, and from it a suitable man is selected to perform their simple and not very frequent religious ceremonies. He is paid and maintained by the rest for doing so, and is exempted from all manual labour so long as he continues to hold the office. The principal festival of their calendar is an annual one, lasting for several days, and held apparently for the purpose of invoking prosperity for their manufactures and tillage.

As with the Jews, the Kaffirs, and many savage races, as well as with the Celts of old, the new moon is observed as a season of festival. Once a year at this time, the different trades of the village bring to the temple an offering of their first-fruits, each presenting a specimen of his own craft, being the first article manufactured in the commencing year. After this, a feast (to which every family in the place has previously been called on by the priest to contribute) is held in the temple with many introductory forms. A general dance takes place after dark round a blazing fire to the music of pipes and tom-toms. It was a striking scene to witness these wild-looking half-naked figures gesticulating and singing round the brightly blazing pile, clapping their hands in time to the fantastic dance.

In reference to this ancient custom of dancing at particular changes of the moon, I cannot resist quoting the following extract from Strabo, given in Col. Forbes-Leslie's *Early Races of Scotland*:

"The Celtiberians sacrifice to a nameless god every full moon at night, before their doors, the whole family passing the night in dancing and festival." This exactly describes the above scene, as well as many similar ones that I have witnessed among the races of South Africa.

Besides their modern temples there are some very interesting carved stones in different parts of the Hills which have apparently been erected at distant epochs. These most probably belong to this race, seeing that they are the only hill-people acquainted with the use of tools.

I accidentally discovered a very curious and perfect object of this character, and of evident antiquity, when shooting at the head of the Khotagiri Pass. In searching for a quail which had fallen into a dense bit of jungle, through which it was difficult to make a way, I came suddenly on a beautiful *kistvaen*, or perhaps *dolmen*, for it partook of the characters of each. It consisted of several large vertical slabs forming three sides of an oblong square, and having others laid horizontally on the top as a roof. It was divided by a centre slab into two cells, or compartments, the whole interior, that is to say, the inner face of each slab, being covered over with carving. The nature of these has now completely escaped my memory, and unfortunately a carefully-made sketch which I took at the time was afterwards lost in the Mysore country, together with my collection of portraits of the different hill-tribes; and of Toda songs and traditions. The latter, written in German, had been kindly presented to me by Mr. Metz, who had collected them among the natives.

Referring to these carved stones, it may not be out of place here to remind you of the eastern character of some of the symbols found on the incised monoliths in our own country; the elephant, for instance, being one frequently met with in Scotland.

The Khotas, unlike their aristocratic neighbours, who all rank equal in the social scale, are of different individual degrees of wealth, and consequent consideration. The funeral rites of the poorer are of necessity of a very simple character, the body being burned by the friends without ceremony, and the ashes forthwith buried. When a well-to-do Khota dies, the body is placed on the funeral pyre with some form, and the ashes are at the end of the year collected by the friends and carried in procession to the place of sepulture, the final honours very much resembling those in vogue among the Todas.

The Kurumbas.—About two-thirds of the way down the mountain sides, which at that height are encircled by a continuous belt of forest, we find the Kurumbas, the third of the hill-tribes, properly so called.* They, in their turn, differ widely from both of those that have been described. Their language has a great many words belonging to, and seemingly borrowed from, the Toda, a fact doubtless due merely to their local position midway between that race and the Erulas, whose strange mixture of various low-country languages forms another portion of the Kurumba vo-

* This tribe is of another race from the shepherd Kurumbas, described by Sir Walter Elliot as having a distinct priesthood, and worshipping the god Bhyra. The Nilgiri tribe have neither cattle nor sheep, and, in language, dress, and customs, have no affinity whatever with their namesakes.

cabulary. They have no written character, and their tongue is rather a jargon of corrupted dialects than a language.

It is not to be wondered at that strange and mysterious stories should be circulated and credited of a people whose dwelling is in the recesses of an unhealthy jungle, avoided alike by natives and Europeans, haunted by wild beasts, and all but impenetrable. Seldom visible, even at a distance, they fly from the approach of civilised man with extraordinary agility, slipping over the steepest crags like the monkeys, their companions, and instantaneously disappearing into the forest-depths. I cannot, however, bear out the popular statements, either that "they have their dwelling in the tops of the highest trees," or are "thickly covered with hair." Their chief food is wild roots and berries, or grain soaked in water, with occasional porcupines or polecats. Their dwellings are nothing more than a few branches piled together like heaps of dead brushwood in a plantation, often simply holes or clefts among the rocks. Their clothing is, with the males, a small dirty cloth round the loins; and with the females, a rag thrown on any way that its condition and size render most available.

With no regular supply of food beyond a little patch of millet here and there in some open spot, which receives no other preparation beyond being scratched with a stick before sowing, and with only a few plantains or occasional jack-fruit, their starvation would be at times inevitable, but for certain allowances from the Vadacas in the form of grain, bestowed on them through fear of their supposed demonocracy and power of evil. For example when any of those industrious, but most superstitious of agriculturalists, are about to commence the ploughing of their land, it is absolutely indispensable for good luck that the first furrow should be turned over by a Kurumba, otherwise the evil power at his command might be let loose to blight the expected crop. The wily savage, who, though evincing an extraordinary respect for the lordly Toda, despises the more wealthy Vadaca, is cunning enough to encourage the dread and secret dislike, in which he sees that he is held, the former owing to his strange immunity from the jungle fever and wild beasts, so dreaded by others, and the latter to his own repulsive personal appearance. He accordingly demands, as a preparatory sacrifice, a calf, or a goat, or a cock, according to the means of the occupier of the land, thus enhancing the solemnity of the ceremony to his own profit. A quantity of the native porridge being made for the occasion is also partaken of by all present. In return for the important protection supposed to be conferred by the foregoing rites, the neglect of which the Vadacas consider as certain to entail loss and disaster, and further, in order to ensure fortunate harvest weather, the magical Kurumba is again summoned when the season arrives, to reap the first handful of corn, receiving for his own use a liberal percentage on the crop. The women eke out their miserable existence by collecting gum and wild honey, for which they find a sale among the Hindoos.

The appearance of these rude people is wretched and even disagreeable. Low in stature, they are also ill-made; the complexion is of an unhealthy hue, and their heads are thinly covered with mangy-looking hair. They have bleared eyes, a rather wide mouth, and often projecting teeth. Spare to leanness, there is also a total absence of any apparent muscle, and the arms and legs are as much like black sticks as human limbs.

The tribe is widely scattered round the range, and is believed to number nearly nine hundred. Their religion resembles that of the Hindoos, so far as one can say that they have any religion at all, for they have neither priests nor temples. Their chief god is the popular Rangasawmie, but he receives no further notice than the small and easily-paid attentions of a plantain or a little grain laid before his stone image. No such ceremony as marriage exists among these people, who live together like the brute creation. Their dead are sometimes burned, sometimes buried; in either case, with as little form or trouble as possible. They are, in short, among the most debased types of mankind.

The Erulas.—The Erulas have been mentioned as inhabiting the immense tracts of forest clothing the lower ranges of the Hills, and, in fact, extend nearly to their base; so that they are less strictly hill-tribes than the others, though regarded as such by the inhabitants of the adjoining plains.

In point of numbers, they are rather superior to the last mentioned tribe, and are divided into two hereditarily distinct classes, an upper and a lower, the latter of which comprises the bulk of the people. This division is not in any way connected with their religion, but is altogether a social matter; and it is one the peculiarity of which becomes more striking when we reflect on their degraded and poverty-stricken state, and on the fact that class distinctions, otherwise than for religious reasons, do not prevail among any of their neighbours.

In general appearance, the Erulas are something between the Kurumbas and the Hindoo pariah, but their hair is more abundant than that of the former, and they are altogether less wretched looking specimens of humanity, though by no means either well formed or pleasing in expression. The only appreciable difference between the upper and the lower classes is, that the former are perhaps more frequently decorated with necklaces and bracelets, made of dried berries or of millet straw, and sometimes have large rings of silver in the ears. The dress is similar to that of the Kurumbas.

Their dwellings, though but rough sheds, are a degree or two better than those of the latter; and they provide their idol, Rangasawmie, with a rude shelter from the weather. They have very few religious rites beyond the simple offering made to it, and the occasional sacrifice of a cock to propitiate evil spirits.

This custom is interesting, as having existed from the earliest ages among partially civilised races, in widely separated countries, both of the old and new world. In the East, we find it practised at the present day, as of old, among several wild tribes of India, by the Cingalese and others. Its progress westward is traceable among the Arabs; and, coming to the western limit of Europe, it is found to have existed, not only in the sun worship of the Celts, but to have been practised both in Scotland and Ireland to within a comparatively recent period.

In respect to food, these people fare no better then their half-starved neighbours, the Kurumbas. As they bestow no labour on the ground, simply sowing their grain in a careless manner on any half-cleared patch that offers itself, the produce is naturally not very great, and the little there is, is never harvested nor stored. The daily supply is cut just as required, and so long as any remains they give themselves no care for the future, but consume what they want on the spot, roughly beating out the grain, and parching it in a rude and primitive way on heated stones. At other seasons, their food consists of wild fruits, roots, and berries. In times of drought, these precarious means of subsistence frequently fail them, and many die of starvation: a fact which, nevertheless, fails to teach any lesson of prudence or industry to the survivors. In the monsoon, the tribe is scattered in all directions, each individual seeking his own subsistence without any regard to the rest, begging or stealing, according to circumstances.

The funeral rites, or rather practices, of the Erulas are most singular; but, as I have not witnessed these myself, I can only speak from the description of others. The almost universal Indian custom of cremation is not resorted to at all; but each of the two classes has its peculiar burial-place as follows. Within a hut of considerable size, placed a little apart from the village, is a large and very deep pit dug in the centre of the earthen floor. The opening into this hole is covered over with the trunks of young trees laid close together, side by side, with a mound of earth raised over them. This is removed for the reception of each fresh corpse, which is flung in headlong like that of a dog, without any ceremony or preparation whatever.

Like the Kurumbas, they have no notion of marriage, but

live promiscuously one with the other, save that the two classes keep themselves to themselves.

Both these unfortunate races have doubtless retrograded, mentally and physically, under their long continued endurance of hardship, and are, probably, in a lower and more debased condition at the present day, than ages ago, on their first arrival in the locality.

In conclusion, it is difficult to believe that any of the tribes I have thus endeavoured to describe (excepting, of course, the Vadacas) can be in any way allied to the inhabitants of the plains; whilst it appears almost impossible as regards the Todas, a tribe as distinct from all its various surrounding neighbours as an oasis in the desert. Superior in physique, countenance, and character, free from the inherent thirst for blood so universal among all wild races, and yet brave and courageous, by moral influence alone exercising dominion over larger tribes, exclusively pastoral, practising polyandry, speaking an unknown tongue, believing in an invisible deity,—they stand totally isolated in the very midst of an enormous population of civilised and progressing people, of an utterly different religion; and after, it may be, thousands of years, still retain unchanged their primitive character, and the observance of religious rites and customs practised in prehistoric times.

There is no doubt that all these hill-tribes are aborigines of the peninsula of India, the whole area of which was probably once occupied by them. Some have thought it possible that they may all have been originally of one race; and others have more boldly argued that, even in the extreme instances of the Toda and the Kurumba, the difference in physical character may be attributed to the nature of the regions they respectively inhabit. This is allowing extraordinary power to such influences, and is, moreover, entirely contradicted by actual fact in the case of the Khotas. That tribe, occupying precisely the same regions as the Todas, is as opposite to them in physical character as is the Kurumba. Why, unless originally different, should one tribe have short clustering hair, with bushy beards, while another in the same district has long straight locks, with little or no beard; why should the one tribe be brown, with women fair, and the other have both sexes perfectly black; and what influence of climate could convert a Kurumba's nose into a Roman one?

It is very probable that the two most degraded of these tribes—namely, the Erulas and Kurumbas—were originally one, and that the slight physical differences existing between them may have resulted from the nature of their respective situations and consequent modes of life. The Todas and Khotas, however, can never have been one people; and the characterising differences of the present day must have always been equally marked. The preservation of their respective characteristics may be due to the fact of these tribes having escaped pursuit, or even observation, at the hands of the successive subjugators of the country, owing to the lofty and inaccessible retreat which they selected for themselves in the Nilgiri mountains. The Todas might indeed have been located there in earlier ages, not only previous to the irruption of the Hindoos across the Indus and through the plains of the Deccan, but anterior to the nations that preceded them, and possibly from the earliest ages. The Erulas and Kurumbas, flying thither for refuge, and finding the summit already in possession of a superior people, would naturally shelter themselves in the untenanted solitudes lower down, hiding in the dense forest of the mountain sides as at the present day. Their partial inoculation with the religion and language of neighbouring races seems also to confirm the theory of isolation in respect to the other, and further removed, tribes. In the Todas, therefore, is it not possible that we may have a remnant of one of the earliest races that inhabited Asia; whose rites and customs, if not introduced into Europe by a westward migration, were doubtless analogous to those of the Celts of Britain? May they not be a living link connecting the present with ages of which we still know next to nothing; and in their singular social customs, religious rites, and even personal appearance may we not picture to ourselves, probably with a very near approach to accuracy, the scenes and people of an era coeval with, or even prior to, the stone monuments which on their mountains, as in this land, have excited so much interest and speculation?

The Todas have been, in turn, considered as outcast Jews, Roman colonists, and Celto-Scythians; one writer asks if they could be Aryans, or might not rather be Turanians, and another propounds their affinity to the Tasmanians. I do not presume to advance an opinion on so difficult a subject as this, but have thought it interesting to point out the striking analogy that exists between their rites, customs, and monuments, and those of the Celts of Early Britain, an analogy not unknown to antiquarians. On the other hand, I have drawn attention to the many points of resemblance existing between them and the Kaffirs. The number of these I might have added to, for I have left unnoticed here some with which I was much struck at the time. I have also glanced at the few points they have in common with the Jews of old, and ~~also~~ with the ancient Romans, whose coins have, by the way, been found plentifully in the Deccan.

Though I do not deduce any theory of origin from the above resemblances, they are equally entitled to notice with the former, and may possibly qualify the soundness of conclusions that have been drawn from Celtic analogy.

The real origin of the Todas and Khotas is a question which, if ever to be elucidated, we are not, as yet perhaps, sufficiently acquainted with their language satisfactorily to determine, and I would earnestly recommend the subject to this Society as one worthy of its investigation. There is, in fact, hardly any more inviting field for the anthropologist than that of Hindostan, almost every quarter of which furnishes wild tribes of whose history little is known. There were two others of these which interested me very much, namely, the Brinjarries and the Niadis.

The former are the gypsies of India, a nomadic tribe roaming the Deccan with large herds of bullocks. The lineaments of the white race are plainly visible in their sable countenances. Their dress, too, is a partial approach to that of the European, though the tall handsome women wear very singular armlets, bangles, and necklaces. One of the latter which I procured, will be found worth the inspection of those acquainted with other eastern ornaments of that nature.

The second tribe, that of the Niadis, is of a totally opposite character. They are a wretched people scattered over the low hills and waste districts of Malabar. They are nearly naked, but are only to be seen at some little distance, generally in parties of ten or twelve, and invariably retreat on the approach of strangers. They attracted the attention of my party by howling in the most unearthly tones, from a rising ground several hundred yards from the road. Looking at them through the glass, they were seen to be miserably thin and wretched-looking creatures of the wildest possible aspect. By the advice of a Hindoo *kotwal*, I put down a few *annas* on a rock by the roadside, for which, as soon as we were at a safe distance, they raced down howling and chattering like so many wild beasts.

Cock sacrifice is practised by these people also, and no doubt many interesting customs and rites might be discovered if properly investigated; but I must not digress from my subject. My only reason for thus incidentally mentioning either of these tribes is to show what material exists for inquiry among the tribes of Southern India, whether on the hills or on the plains.

To return for a moment to the former, I may add in conclusion that the Todas and Khotas of the present day are unfortunately degenerating. Both tribes are, I think, naturally capable of considerable improvement, both mentally and morally, but, so far as I saw, and especially in the case of the former, their contact with the European has hitherto produced only its too common results, intoxication, licentiousness, and cupidity, threatening to add to the long list of so-called uncivilised races that the white man has assisted to demoralise.

PRINTED BY T. RICHARDS, 37, GREAT QUEEN STREET, W.C.